It's my FIRST DAY of SCHOOL!

WRITTEN BY
SHARI LAST

It's my first day of school and I have a new backpack.

It's my first day of school
and I will miss my mom.

It's my first day of school and I am a little nervous.

It's my first day of school and
I can't wait to explore the play area!

It's my first day of school and I have a cool classroom.

It's my first day of school and I am going to learn new things.

It's my first day of school and I made a new friend!

It's my first day of school and I got a bit messy!

It's my first day of school and
I like my new teacher.

It's my first day of school and
I am so proud of myself!

It's my first day of school and my big brother comes to say hi.

It's my first day of school and I have so much to tell you!

It's my first day of school and I am so tired!

There is no ONE way to head off to school.
There is no one way to do ANYTHING!

How would you describe yourself?

I am ....

I am ....

I am ....

Write down three things you are excited about on your first day of school!

1.	2.	3.

First published in Great Britain in 2024
Cupcake Press,
an imprint of
TELL ME MORE Books

Text copyright ©2024 Shari Last
Design copyright ©2024 Shari Last

ISBN: 978-1-917200-13-4

Picture credits: Thanks to Adobe Stock.

All rights reserved. Without limiting the rights under the copyright reserved above, no part of this publication may be reproduced, stored in, or introduced into a retrieval system, or transmitted, in any form, or by any means (electronic, mechanical, photocopying, recording or otherwise), without the prior written permission of the copyright owner.

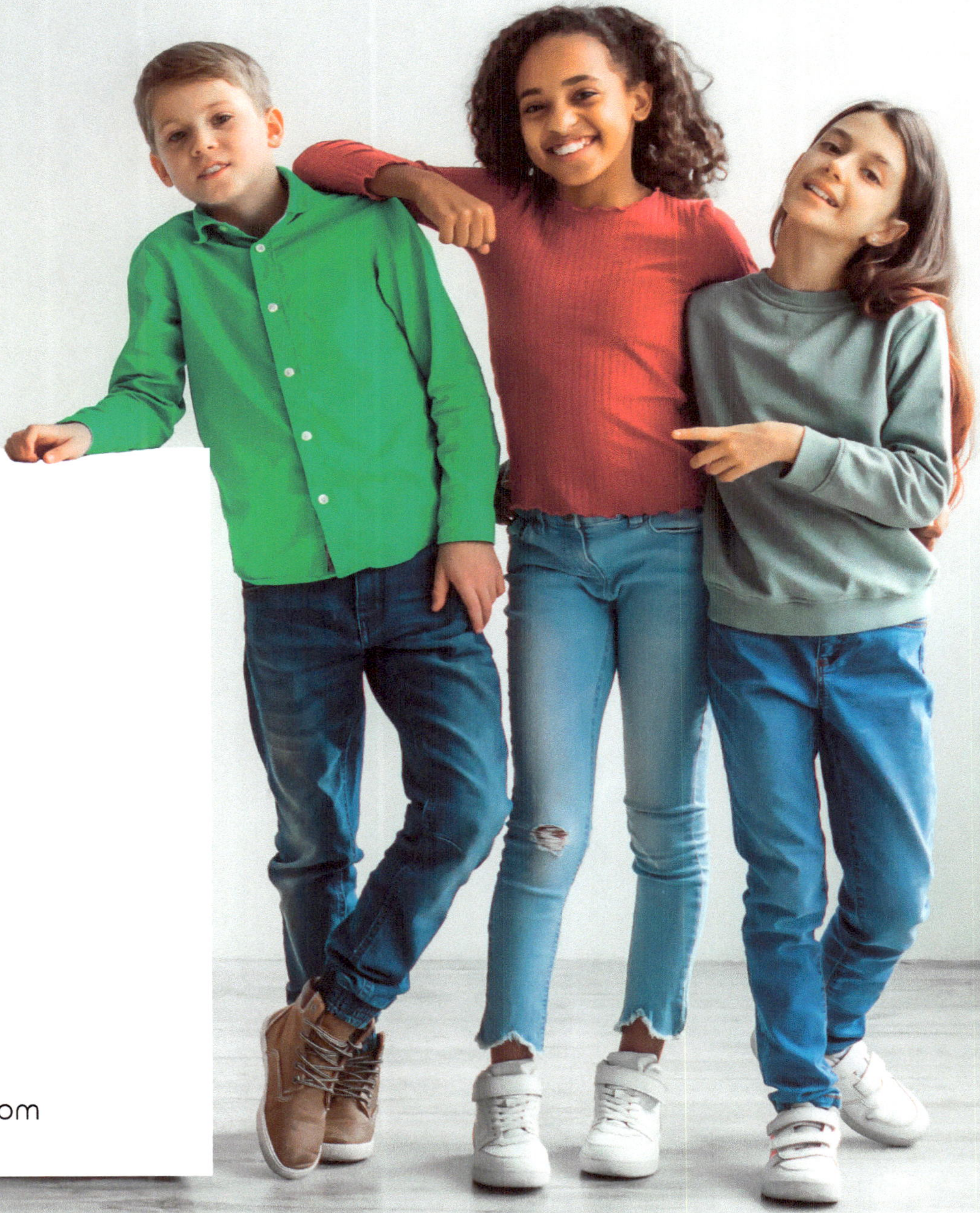

CUPCAKE PRESS

Visit our website:
www.tellmemorebooks.com

www.ingramcontent.com/pod-product-compliance
Lightning Source LLC
Chambersburg PA
CBHW050749110526
44591CB00002B/28